In the Ba...

by Kira Freed

Table of Contents

What Is a Habitat?	4
Why Are Plants Important to a Backyard?	8
Why Are Animals Important to a Backyard?	14
Glossary and Index	20

I need to know these words.

food chain

habitats

insect

pollen

shelter

soil

What Is a Habitat?

A **habitat** is a place with living things. Plants and animals live in habitats. Habitats have nonliving things, too. Rocks, **soil**, and water are in habitats.

Some habitats have large ▶ amounts of water.

▲ Many plants and animals live in this habitat.

Habitats have different types of weather. Some habitats are wet and other habitats are dry. Habitats may be warm or cool. Different things live in different habitats.

◀ Many things live in this wet habitat.

▲ A desert is a dry habitat.

A backyard can be a habitat. A backyard has living and nonliving things. Different backyards have different living things. The weather and soil are also different. We can study backyards to learn about habitats.

◀ **This backyard gets a large amount of rain.**

▲ **The soil in this backyard is sandy.**

Some backyards are in cities. Other backyards are in the country. Backyards may be large or small.

This small backyard ▶ is in a city.

▲ This large backyard is in the country.

Why Are Plants Important to a Backyard?

Plants help other living things in backyards. Some backyards have tall trees. Grass grows in many backyards. Some plants in backyards have flowers. Other plants have fruit. What plants live in your backyard?

▲ Many plants grow in this backyard.

Backyards in different places have different plants. Some plants need water every week. Other plants need water only every few months.

Rain falls on these ▶ plants many days each year.

▲ A cactus can live a long time without water.

Many animals get food from plants. Some animals eat grass or leaves. Other animals eat nuts or berries. Some animals drink the juice of flowers.

◀ **This squirrel eats nuts from plants.**

▲ **This hummingbird drinks juice from flowers.**

Many animals use plants for **shelter**. Birds make nests in trees. Raccoons also live in trees. **Insects** use hollow logs as homes.

Many animals use plants to hide from other animals. Plants keep animals safe from bad weather, too.

**This bird is safe ▶
in a tree.**

▲ **This log is home for many insects.**

Soil is important in a backyard. Plants sink their roots into soil.

Worms make tunnels in soil. The tunnels add air to the soil. The air helps plants grow better.

◀ Roots grow deep into soil.

▲ Worms are good for soil and plants.

Many people have gardens in their backyards. Flowers and vegetables grow in gardens. Flowers make a backyard more beautiful. People eat the vegetables. Gardens bring more animals to backyards.

▲ People grow flowers so that butterflies will visit.

◀ Insects visit gardens. Birds visit to eat the insects.

Why Are Animals Important to a Backyard?

Some animals help other living things in backyards. Tiny animals live in soil. Backyards have insects and spiders. Some of these animals are food. What animals live in your backyard?

◀ A person found this turtle in a backyard.

▲ This backyard has a lizard.

Some animals help plants grow. These animals drink the juice of flowers. **Pollen** gets on the animals' bodies. Pollen is special powder that flowers make. The animals carry pollen to other flowers. Then the flowers can make seeds. The seeds grow into new plants.

Pollen is on ▶ this bee.

◀ Butterflies help flowers make seeds.

Backyards have **food chains**. Food chains show how animals get food. Food chains start with plants. Some animals eat plants. Some animals eat other animals. Some animals eat plants and other animals.

All living things in a backyard need one another. Some animals help plants make seeds. Some animals spread the seeds of plants.

Some animals eat many insects. These animals stop insects from eating all the plants.

◀ This bat helps plants make seeds.

▲ Insects are food for this bird.

Cats change backyards. Cats hunt animals in backyards. Cats kill many birds in backyards. Cats kill mice and squirrels, too. Backyards have more animals if cats stay inside.

▲ This cat caught a bird in a backyard.

Try giving seeds to birds. Put the seeds in a special place. Do more birds come to the backyard? What can you do to bring animals to your backyard?

◀ This bird eats special seeds in a backyard.

▲ These birds take a bath in a backyard.

Glossary

food chain (FOOD CHANE): the order in which living things pass energy
See page 16.

habitats (HA-buh-tats): the places where animals, plants, or people live
See page 4.

insect (IN-sekt): an animal that has six legs and a body with three parts
See page 11.

pollen (PAH-lun): special powder that a flower makes
See page 15.

shelter (SHEL-ter): a place that provides safety
See page 11.

soil (SOIL): material that covers Earth's surface
See page 4.

Index

animals, 4, 10–11, 13–19
cats, 18
food chain, 16
garden, 13
habitats, 4–6
insect, 11, 13–14, 17

plants, 4, 8–12, 15–17
pollen, 15
shelter, 11
soil, 4, 6, 12, 14
water, 4, 9